AFTER THE ACCIDENT

❖

JOHN SAUNDERS

❖

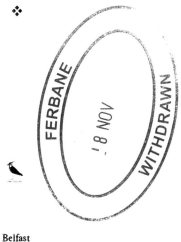
Belfast
LAPWING

First Published by Lapwing Publications
c/o 1, Ballysillan Drive
Belfast BT14 8HQ
lapwing.poetry@ntlworld.com
http://www.freewebs.com/lapwingpoetry/

ACKNOWLEDGEMENTS

Thank you to the editors of the following publications where some of the
poems in this collection first appeared.
The Sharp Review, Riposte, The Unitarian Church Newsletter,
The Smoking Poet.

A special thanks also to poets Jean O' Brien and Rita Ann Higgins who have
given me enormous support and encouragement in my endeavours.

Set in Aldine 721 BT at the Winepress

ISBN 978-1-907276-26-2

ii

CONTENTS

DEDICATION

For Dympna, Jack and James.

AFTER THE ACCIDENT

When we got there she was dead,
her face now pale
her lips relaxed, at last.
They had tried as best they could
to clean away the blood;
to spare our feelings I suppose.
In that cold room, I wished
for her, a peaceful repose.
As we left, I remembered
her kisses on my head.

AMBITION

It is, as it was, mesmerising.
The jugglers are juggling,
the clowns clowning.

Marfanic girls, contorted like
flying yogi's, swing upside down
in the cranium of the tent

and in the ring is a small boy
the height of a horse's nostril
riding bareback on a stallion,

his hands pointing to the sky,
as if to say – *someday,*
I too will swing at the top.

ANCESTORS

I can see them now
on the cold horizon
of the untouched landscape.

They trundle along
in their skins
carrying all they own,

some flint, a heavy
stick, wild berries.
Enough for now.

If I look closely
I can see their faces,
those familiar lines

as they seek shelter
to protect their legacy
and my heritage.

BLISS
After Raymond Carver

He drank to escape, from what
he could not be sure. It was
not like you imagine, staggering,
puking, blackouts, instead,
a slow descent into an abyss.
First evening, then lunchtime,
morning and the middle of the night.
The signs were there, days gone amiss,
memory loss, friends lost, ambitions
abandoned, soaked in piss.
Everybody said *stop* except him.
There was no way back only forward
through the opacity of bliss.

ATHENS 2008

I am in the city of wisdom
within spitting distance of that place
where Archimedes displaced the water
and streaked.
Where Heraclites saw everything change
and Socrates and Plato asked
the difficult questions
and got no answers.

The same city where Diogenes,
the cynic lived, in a barrel,
and Aristotle pondered the big issues.
That self same city where
Homer began his odyssey
and Euripides and Sophocles
spun out their tragedies.

This sacred rock of crumbling temples
and olive trees stands,
proud of its history, amidst the din
of the twenty first century
circling around its feet
in true Pythagorean style

How juxtaposed the two
worlds stand. The first
long dead, yet its lessons live,
the other dying
having not yet learned.

YUGGERA

You dance to commemorate, to celebrate
the change in your world.

You walk to meet, to greet
your tribal friends.

You sing to communicate, to locate
your natural land.

You make fire, you inspire
with your primal ways

You show for us, your exodus
from the sacred ground.

You breathe into the seed
of human survival.

You display your indignity
With your primordial dignity.

ON SHARING A TABLE WITH AN IBIS

It was when he perched on the side
of my table that I realised there are
still things I do not know.
This puffy bird with the sabre like beak
audaciously searching for crumbs,
looks me straight in the eye.
How quickly I move to protect my store.
He sits as if to say, *May I join you?*
I nod and hold tightly my cup of coffee.

SOUVENIRS

A Gecko leg key ring, a Crocodile head totem
an Emu's claw back-scratcher or a Kangaroo's Scrotum.

How must the animal spirits in their dreaming
think, to know they are now a tourist plaything.

Perhaps, they feel like their human counterparts,
unselfish donors of now useless body parts.

Heroes of modern medicine and victims of tourism
can rest in peace knowing that they have given

to their grateful companions on this earth
new life and delight from their unfortunate death.

BUSY

He is sitting at his desk busy
sorting notes, letters, messages.
He has no time to spare.
There since dawn, not leaving
until dark, he will sort
pile, file, bin and prioritise
the mass of information,
yesterday on some one
else's desk, tomorrow
on another until he retires.
Then there is gardening, golf,
walks, daytime TV, art and pottery
hospital appointments, his
last illness.

BASTARD

You dragged me down
like a drowning man, digging
his nails in so, that I bled.

Even now, I bear the scars,
healed, but still hurting,
reminding me of you.

Sleepless, I lie, thinking
of how I let you fool me,
trick me like a child.

Even with the fog of time
I cannot forget you nor
forgive. You bastard,

it is a wonder to me
that I am here in one piece.
Despite your intent

I have survived, like a wild
flower in a poisoned field.

BIBLIOPHILIA

I remember well the taste
off the paper of the older ones.
Musty pages, yellowed,
turned down corners, pencilled
underlines. Evidence of
use and abuse.

They stood, spines upright,
showing their titles.
Aristocrats of knowledge,
ordered by Dewey, the more
learned ones, referring
only to us.

We raced home, grasping
the heavy tomes, our minds
infected by these fomites.
Our whole lives ahead of us,
the possibility of death
bound in our hands.

CASTRO

On the morning Castro retired,
I walked up Grafton Street,
the mounds of blankets
lying still in disused doorways.

In Havana, I imagined,
there are blankets in doorways.
Dictatorship or not
the hovels look the same.

CHANGE

What is this change? An end or a beginning?
An end to the articulation of desire,
a stepping back from unforgiving demand,
from the unflinching testament of imperfection.

A beginning of something, the possibility
of the self, like a tree budding in springtime,
a blade of grass reawakening in a new light
unshaped by rigorous obligation.

A time to fly above the solid earth
like a swallow fleeing winter into the blue
of endless perfection, free to return
only when the seasons rotate again.

There is a lesson, a note of advisement.
Be like the budding tree, the reawakened blade
of grass, the fleeing swallow. Do not remain
the same until the dictator of time calls.

CLOUDS ON THE GROUND

you remark, as we stare
at our fogbound garden.
Your observation shakes me
to the realisation that you
are unbound by rules.
You demonstrate the liberty
of the young mind, still
pliant, ready to absorb.
Recovering, I look at you
and seek in vain a response
to match your wisdom.

CHILDREN PLAYING IN THE GRAVEYARD

The dead shall never hear
them laughing as they cheer

and trespass from mound to mound
oblivious to the sacred ground,

in front of them a journey
endless and without turning.

Too young to know otherwise,
they do not see with adult eyes

the dark corners of the world,
the harsh lives of the old.

They will not know the weight of sadness,
the gut burn of hopelessness,

until the illusion of immortality
is broken by earthly brutality,

leaving them to realise
the fragility of their single lives.

After the Accident

CONCEPTION

Last year I had no idea of you.
You were not even a rough draft

until that early morning in September
when you came in the rising before the day begins.
That time when light creeps around the curtains
to find a place to land and be there when you stir.

It's as if you quietly slipped under the duvet,
your partly dressed body cosying up to me.
I could just make out your shape, feel your feminine verbs
move, touch your similes and half rhymes.
If I squinted my eyes I could even see your unfinished lines.

Tempted , I embraced you to explore your metaphors
and soften them to gentle rhythms. I caressed your
stanzas into perfect forms that could stand alone.
Then, when you were responding to my advances,
I filled you with imagination until you could take no more,
And left you alone to face the world in your completeness.

DEATH OF A PRINCESS

They gutted
and left her to dry. Then,
they packed and oiled
her body and wrapped
it in soft cloth.

Secured now in death
they coffined it twice
and buried it with gifts,
food, precious stones,
gold, her favourite pet.

I see the Gods now,
unravelling the oiled
cotton, revealing her porcelain
body. They envelope her
in their Godly arms and soar

high above the stone tomb,
over the ancient flat earth
into the tuat, a place
not yet known. A principality
of the eternal journey.

DOCTOR

he is the scholar who reads our history
he is the postman who delivers on birthdays
he is the explorer who looks into our caves
he is the conductor who listens to the sounds we make
he is the policeman who cautions us to slow down
he is the tailor who mends our cloth
he is the weatherman who warns us of storms on the way
he is the priest who hears our confessions

he is the pusher who satisfies our need for drugs
he is the judge who incarcerates us against our will
he is the leech who takes our blood
he is the victualler who makes clean cuts
he is the fireman who attends the scene of our accidents
he is the stationmaster who tells when we depart.

MURPHY

Down winding streets I walk
as straight as a die
afraid to look, in case
he is there.

He shouts across the street
startling me to run.
I glance back and spy his frame.
Murphy is out again.

EARTH MOVEMENTS

There was an earthquake today in Donegal,
two point four on the scale.
The earth relieving itself.
The geo-scientists, agitated
as tectonic plates,
study the seismograph with glee;
observing the shifting continental shelf.

In Killibegs, Mrs Gallagher, shook,
worries about the slates
and adjusts the sacred heart on the wall.
Sweeping brush at the ready
she trembles and weeps over the remains
of the Beleek vase.
A wedding present.
The cat slips under the sofa,

smooth as lava.
The radio assures us
it was not sumanigenic.
Thanks be to God, she whispers,
crossing herself, as she
sweeps the broken delph
and shoos the cat out
into the dangerous night.

EARTHRISE

Look at that picture over there.
Look again at that blue dot, a lonely
speck in the great envelope of dark,
a place of warmth and life in a desert
of deathly coldness. *Isn't that something?*

In our obscurity, in all the vastness
there is no hint that help will come
from elsewhere to save ourselves.
That is the only home we have,
our only space in space.

On it, everyone we love, everyone
we know, everyone we have
ever heard of. Every human being who is.
All that was happened there.
Behold earthrise.

BETRAYAL

I suppose it had to happen.
You would finally betray me,
showing your feet of clay.

For six years or more
I have adored you,
as you shaped my life.

You replenished my soul.
Your mantra of love and light
echoed around my head.

Now, it transpires,
you have exposed your humanity
and broken my heart.

EMILY MURPHY SAYS WOMEN ARE PERSONS TOO
The Persons Case 1928, Canada

She wished to be the first elected
and was prevented by laws enacted.
The Supreme Court held its view
that women were not persons too.
She cried *no* as the judges' rose
their verdicts now disclosed.

Not wishing to wait for reform
she set her sights on the English Crown.
The all male members of the Privy Council
on appeal listened to her codicil
and declared amidst the hullabaloo
that women were in fact persons too.

COMMERCE

I am on the eight thirty five with the whirl
of commerce about me.
My pinstriped companion
is whispering to his dictaphone.
Across the aisle a young girl
is face booking the world.
The rest are minding their own business
while I am looking out at the racing fields
and wondering what the next line
of this poem might be.

END

A small term to mean the stopping of everything.
One syllable marks the final point before nothing,
like when the film is over, that single word,
or the square on the edge of the games board.
When the curtains close on the empty stage,
when months give way to years and we age
until the last day is unknowingly reached
and it is time to move on to a place unsearched.

With people too there is a time for separation
when their journey has come to completion.
All living things become unfeasible
and we must then succumb to the inevitable.
No matter how greatly we pretend
we all face the same fate in the end.

FEAR

And it is fear that drives me.
Fear of not achieving all that I want to,
of being left behind,
in the gutter of life.
I am not quite there yet, but close,
as I rim the edges of chance,
while around me the fences fall
exposing me to the blades of failure.

EYES WIDE OPEN

You stand, eyes wide open,
between the two seats staring,
transported to the ecstasy
of mid flight, soaring above
the white spume, over the arc
of the indifferent earth.

He explains, how the wheel
steers, letting you manoeuvre
with your small hands, one hundred
and eighty eight tons of aircraft
 home, to bring us safely down
on solid ground, to our roots.
Grounded.

HANGING FROM THE MOON

From where I stand it looks like an earring
hanging from the ear of the crescent moon.
I imagine the shiny aluminium ship, locked
in orbit, silent, in the empty endless space,
its surface glistening in the solar light.

 The shining jewel of the universe blinks
in the black sky, a watchful eye peering
over the horizon of the heavy earth
like a mother watching her small baby
as it rolls towards certain danger.

FAREWELL
i.m. of Jim Greely

It's those eyes that always got me,
that mischievous look.
You could eye me up,
but not in a threatening way.
More like, *great to see you*.

I knew when you were about.
Prattling, full of bonhomie,
the life and soul of the party.
That devilish smile of gay abandon,
as you posed, cigarette in hand.

Inside the rogue, beat
a Samaritans heart.
An ear for every woe,
an agony aunt for every party,
always ready to corroborate.

You scoundrel.
You have robbed us of your fun
and life has lost its best fan.
farewell my friend,
party in peace.

FLASHBACK

The glances of strangers show
your eyes, burning with passion,
as you come to me.

It happens at most peculiar times.
An off the cuff remark, rolls me
back to middle of the night

whispers of lust.
The kisses of strangers
recall me to your red lips

on the verge of ecstasy.
The flavour of soft fruit juices,
rekindles the taste of your mouth

wetting mine.
The scent of showered bodies,
flashbacks me, to you
washing the spillage of seed away.

FLOOR BOARDS

I am standing there holding the battens,
a child apprentice to the master craftsman,
as he lines up the tongue to the groove
careful to make seamless the joins.

Each length is poised and pinned
into place, not to be removed again.
Before the final piece, a familiar ritual,
names on paper tucked into the space.

Those who walk across these boards.
will not know who laid them there.
Only the spirits of the workers remain
in the secret signatures underfoot.

GLENBARROW

I am walking with you in this place of half light
on undulating ground carpeted in its own history.
Beside us, the river follows its course
led by the cut of rock and soft sand.
It flows, gurgling and foaming to its own end.

When we reach the glistening waterfall,
we stand, listening to the noise and rage of nature
hammering the table of the earth. Spears of light
strike the soaked rocks and are thrown to the wet
 ground. We are on nature's battlefield.

Around us stand the columns of conifers
stretching their heads for the kiss of the sun,
shadowing the cool ground of their roots.
They are sentries of this valley, the guardians
 of its riches, found and unfound.

To leave this place is to journey from
the feral , virginal and unclaimed,
to the spoilt splurge of our humanity.
We do so in silence, both of us secretly wishing
that we could stay a little longer, alone.

GIRL TAKING A PHOTOGRAPH OF HERSELF

Ruckling her lips, as if to kiss,
she smoothes the fresh lipstick
with her porcelain finger,
as gentle as a cotton bud.

Holding the phone at arm's length
she smiles and shoots herself.
Up close, she studies the image,
proofing for blemishes, before
saving and sending with an X.

HOLOCAUST

In the death like cold of the night
the train rolls, iron tracks rumble.
They tremble, frozen with fright.

Skin and bone, they stand, tight,
crushed inside wagons as they tumble
in the death like cold of the night.

They huddle and pray, bowed contrite,
that their God may hear every mumble.
They tremble, frozen with fright.

Some whisper and chant with all their might,
some search for crumbs, as they fumble
in the death like cold of the night.

The engines halt, out of sight,
their cargo spills out, hopes crumble.
They tremble, frozen with fright.

Slowly, they end their last flight,
hungry and weak, some stumble
in the death like cold of the night.
They tremble, frozen with fright.

I REMEMBER

I remember her scurrying like a mole.
That craggy faced nun,
fisting a wooden ruler, coif
pinned into her head,
mouth puckered like a sphincter.
Her wimple as white as her soul.

I remember the closed yard,
walled, dark, the green painted doors
keeping us, at once, in and out.

I remember the darkness of the grounds,
taking over the day, over us.
The cut of the March wind
burning bare legs. Our thighs
chaffed on short pants, as harsh
as the ruler on cold young hands.

I FEEL SAD

When I meet
a child, delicate
and fresh, like a new shoot
replacing the old about
to fall to the ground
at the first cut of
Autumn frost,
I feel sad.

John Saunders

I HAVE NOT WALKED THE GREAT WALL OF CHINA

I have not walked the Great Wall of China
and looked over its back at the vastness of Mongolia

or climbed the Statue of Liberty
and viewed from her crown the sadness of her city.

I have not scaled Ramesses at Luxor
and marvelled from his lap at the colossal structure,

nor stepped the weathered stones to the Acropolis
and looked into the minds of the ancient philosophers.

What I have done is looked into your brown eyes
 and soared high into the endless skies,

listened to your words of love in my ears
and heard the wisdom of a thousand years,

felt your warm touch against my hand
and dreamt of great journeys across the land.

IMAGINE

Today I saw an elephant painting
gentle strokes on a blank canvas.
I stare, intrigued, at the genius
of our fellow creatures.

The ants that design and build
unassisted by computers.
The spider who weaves silk
without a loom. A salmon

who swims back to his birthplace
devoid of map or compass and
underground the worms who
can replicate without sex.

And I imagine the artists out there.
The opera singing horses,
the tap dancing giraffe,
the poetry reciting rabbits.

INNOCENCE

Past Keyser's lane we hopped and skipped.
Happy in our innocence, we swapped
sweet kisses and pledged our troth.

I remember your long straight hair
falling to your waist,
the static lifting single strands,
your soft Newry voice whispering
the promises of untarnished youth.

Is your hair untouched
where ever you are now?

IN THE MIDDLE OF THE NIGHT

In the middle of the night
you stroke my face,
your gentle breath
warms my shoulder,
your wispy hair
tickles my cheek.

In that sacred time
the world is still.
Nothing moves but
your heart and the
hands of the clock.

Both marking time.

You, warm and safe
shielded, even from the
ghosts of your dreams.

ISJUHY

This morpheme has no residency in any of the great lexicons
of the English tongue, or any other for that matter.

No philologist or linguist could extract a meaning
or discover a root in the ancient tree of the classics

nor could it be found in a sentence or title, except, on this poem.
The word, if indeed it is one, can only have meaning

for you and I. For you, as you stack the alphabet blocks,
it is your opening gift to the argot of your inheritance,

for me, trying to read the letters before the tower falls,
it is your first written communiqué.

A VILLANELLE FOR JOHN BARRY

John Barry stands guard over this tumbling down town,
looking eastwards for invaders on the high seas.
They say he sank twenty ships that belonged to the Crown.

The estuary gleams, as it reflects the morning sun.
Dockers and sailors assemble on the North quays.
John Barry stands guard over this tumbling down town.

When the tide moves in, the boats prepare to sail on
for the mainland of Europe and to the East Indies,
where it's said he sank twenty ships that belonged to the Crown.

When the sun is in the west and the day moves to sundown,
the quayside is cooled by a south easterly breeze,
John Barry stands guard over this tumbling down town.

All is quiet in the town as night time comes down.
Women gather to chat, with children on their knees,
of how he sank twenty ships that belonged to the Crown.

The moon rises high and the women are all gone.
The shops are shut up, the men home from the factories.
John Barry stands guard over this tumbling down town.
They say he sank twenty ships that belonged to the Crown.

LOVE NOTE NUMBER ONE

A kiss is always a discovery,
lips exploring the intimate.
A smile is sometimes a light
shining in the night of sadness.
An embrace brings warmth,
a blanket against the cold air.
A whisper of love gives faith
like the murmur of a prayer.
The gentle touch of a hand
soothes the anxious mind.
The sound of a familiar breath
blows away the scent of death.

LOVE NOTE NUMBER TWO

My rough hand kneads your soft belly
undulating in counter to your breath.
We are warmed by each other. I can smell
you, feel your hair, sense your trusting body
fold into my lap as if I am the mould
and you the molten pouring into me,
to shape and set. Pure gold, precious,
not for barter, safe. Forever.

LOVE NOTE NUMBER THREE

I can smell the scent of love
in the air as the winds speaks to me
telling me of good times, blowing
its full force, singing it's life.
My face is reddened from its blast,
 my skin warmed by the advance.
After the wind it is cold.
Sometimes, good comes
 after bad, as wind is followed
by an awful calm.

LOVE NOTE NUMBER FOUR

It felt like a kiss, except, in its place
 your fingertips on my neck
brushing against my cold skin

as I imagined you standing behind me
enclosing me in your powerful arms,
sheltering me from the sharp wind.

I searched for your hands to hug
me and grasped the air
that filled your absent space.

Each day gets harder and harder
as I go on without you near me.
Go on to my uncertain future.

LOVE NOTE NUMBER FIVE

Out of the mist you arrive
eyes sparkling like ice,
the colour of Maple.

We have coffee on the corner
of Metcalfe and Slater,
your smile melting my heart

as you open yourself
to me and I to you.
The swordplay of the mind.

Our parting is sweetened
by the taste of your lips
on mine as you fade away.

FIRST TIME

The first time we fucked,
you asked for coffee.

As I prepared it, you remarked,
in your casual way, how relaxed
I was, standing there, naked.

You told me, I would never
be loved as much again.
I did not believe you then.

That night, the weather forecast.
A depression from the West,
the outlook gloomy.

LOVE PLAY

You come to me without warning
slipping into my unplanned life.
Gate crashing my show.

You dance across my life's stage
like a single dying swan.
The spotlight on you.

You play the lead role
in my tragedy, shooting me
with your romantic lines.

You haunt the balconies
of my heart, the lights dimmed,
the doors closed.

And finally you slip away
exiting under the backdrop
as the curtain falls.

TRICK OF LOVE

You laughed teeth gleaming in the light of day,
your hair backcombed and set
and your good earrings, a birthday present.

Your face is full of awe, full of love, for him.
his presence lights you up and warms your heart
you know he will always be there.

LOVE TIME

I sit in the dark, listening
to the clock, tick tocking,
passing the time with sureness,
aging the world and us.
I think of you

in that twilight time,
the bridge between day and
night, when the eye
is fooled by tricks of light,
and darkness falls.
I think of you,

as dusk closes in,
shedding the day and fall
to sleep floating across
the world of dreams.
My love for you
growing beyond belief.

MADEIRA

Virgin Mary blue sky
stretches into the distance,
before falling to the sea

as the sun pours down
like a volcano
on my burning skin.

Petrified lava
roasts my soles
as I stand watching you.

You are my rock.

MEADOW FLOWERS

On the shelf in front of me, the blurb
promises me a meadow of flowers.
Ox Eye Daisies, Black Eyed Susans, Musk Mallow
and Cornfield Annuals drape the front
of the packet in a motley fresco.
I am absorbed into them, trampling
over the sweet smelling hill, my feet whipping
through the grasses of Timothy, Fescue,
Brown Top Bent and Crested Dog tail.
I am falling into the ocean of blooms,
their heads stretching into the sun,
their stems dancing the rhythm of the breeze.
I want to live and die in my meadow,
to soften into the very ground, feed
the flower giving soil, become those flowers,
the scented foliage under your feet
as you come looking for me over
that vast expanse of sensuous wilderness.

MODELS

She is wearing only her perfect hair.
There is no curtsy to modesty,
her uncovered body glowing
under the angled lights. I can
see the perfect ovals of her breasts.
Her friend is there too, wide eyed,
staring at the moon of the ceiling,
audacious in her nakedness.
There are others, less perfect,
one without arms, another
headless. They are also naked,
their still bodies posed obtusely,
captured in the cold frame.
Outside those who pass are
mesmerised for a moment
before moving on into the
darkness of the night.

THIS IS HOW IT ENDS

This is how it ends.
The final rite of passage.
A life complete,
a purpose found.

A priest will be kind
throw soil to the ground
and speak prayerful words
to those left behind.

The rest of the tearful day
will be talking and drinking,
remembering this and that,
of no importance now

as the shroud is spread
and the moon hurls itself
over the cold earth
saying goodbye to the dead.

PAUL NEWMAN IS DEAD

It was a week before I knew he was dead.
I still don't know which one he played.
What I do know is that he found
pleasure in giving.
What I also know is that his
mayonnaise flavoured the lives of
children all over the world.

PURGE

I feel the needles of discontent
pierce me one by one,
as I read and reread until
I can look at you no more.

I am no longer pleased with
your bulging lines, your
excursions into the plains
of the margins, your wanderings
over the road of meaning.

I cannot stand over the pallid
images of nothing happening,
the reservoir of stagnant rhyme,
the clichéd turns of phrase.

I need you to slap my face,
to creep up and frighten
the very wits that made you.
 To drive out the demons
of indolence and cant.

I want to hold the edge
of creativity's knife until
 the blood stains every page
 of our wretched lives.

ON VISITING THE UNITARIAN CHURCH
IN STEPHEN'S GREEN

In this place where dead soldiers are commemorated in brass
I sit and contemplate its sacred past.
All eyes are on the pulpit. More Victorian Gothic.
In the first pew, the hymnals, stacked like stone,
are long untouched. Their redundancy is plain.

In this place of unity and adoration
I imagine its busy days of morning service,
Evening prayer, Sunday school and Thanksgiving.
I wonder how many souls have passed through here,
have sung and prayed for mercy and salvation.

In this place of asymmetrical corners,
founded by heretical dissenters, all are equally welcome
to share their unity of faith in the hope of new beginnings.
As I rise to leave, I am reminded of the dead soldiers,
commemorated on these cold walls.

ONE

Our eyes see each other
watching the same sights.

Our ears hear us
listening to the same sounds.

Our hands touch our bodies
sensing our own presence.

Our nostrils capture our scent
inhaling both of us.

Our tongues taste each of us
savouring our flavours.

We breathe the same air.
We are one.

ORYX AND CRAKE
after the book by Margaret Atwood

Snowman
scavenging and hoarding,
stockpiling
at the world's end.

No more supermarket trips,
microwave dishes.
 gone, TV game shows,
pre-prandial drinks.
Gone, neatly pressed dry cleaned clothes.

Instead, chilling winds,
radiated crops.
Starving dogs, rabid and howling.
Acid filled clouds,
dust storms without warning.
What now of
Oryx and Crake.

LOSS

Your glassy tear filled eyes
tell me all I need to know.
Your sad toned voice
speaks volumes of your thoughts.
Your ashen and weary face
displays your trauma to the world.
In life he was your soul mate,
in death, he is now
a grief ravaged memory.

PADDY KINSELLA'S HAND

In Paddy Kinsella's work room
the air is filled with dust,
blinding like a sandstorm.
His bony figure barely visible

as he presses the pencilled
template to the blade, guiding
with one hand until
the chosen shape appears

and then chisel a tenon
to join timber to timber,
bevel to bevel, as one.
Seamlessly formed.

I am prompted to wonder
on the greatness of such skill
that can shape from Oak
or Teak such ornate work,

a turned leg, a polished table
a child's toy, a simple stand,
nurtured from the cradle
of master craft; now lost

to flat packed veneer,
racked in warehouses
everywhere, untouched
by his hand.

PICTURE

A moment captured from
the harshness of the time,
that picture has haunted me
for forty years or more.

The younger ones, scrubbed and posed,
the rest trying to look older.
A sofa of brown leather
covered for the occasion.

Something in the back of my mind
tells me it was a Sunday morning
and the sun shone through
the front window. It was as if

heaven cast its light on us.
I cannot remember now, what
this holy family did
for the rest of the day.

OBITUARIES

Sitting in post operative
splendour I shake
my anaesthetised foot
at the world and listen
to the obituaries on the radio.

Poor Mrs O Brien
has passed away peacefully
after a long illness, borne bravely.
We should be grateful
for the short time we have,
while we can.

PIRATES

Guns replace swords.
The skull and crossbones,
a Caribbean myth
in the mind of a child.
These seas, now home to
ocean liners, enchant
old money and new,
safe above deck,
sipping sun downers.

In Somalia, desperate
men in boats raid for ransom.
The press reports
of pirates on the
coast of Africa,
are of trivial interest
to the handsome passengers
alighting in St Kitts.

MR TAXI MAN

The Lyric FM listening taxi driver
waxes lyrical about the damaged railing.
Seven years it's been like that,
politicians of every hue use that queue
and still no one with a screwdriver.
It's a joke.
Mozart wafts gently over the airwaves
beautiful horn concertos compete
with Mr. taxi man.
I listen,
spoilt for choice.

PLEADINGS

i

Stop and listen to the silence.
Try not to hear familiar sounds,
instead, close your ears

to the radio, the hum
of the fridge, even the comforting
sound of purring phones.

Stop listening to your own sound,
your heartbeat, the fall of your breath,
the rush of your blood.

Listen to the silence around you,
to the sound of nothing.
You might hear something.

ii

Stay a while with me
and listen, you might learn.
Stay with me and look,

you might see something.
Stay and we might learn
together. Stay with me.

iii

Look out and see
what might be there.
Do not be blinded

by light or dark. Sit and look
as far as you can see
and watch the vista

of possibility unfold
before your eyes.
See the shape of the future.

POEM FOR AN ANNIVERSARY

If I were fire
I would warm your hands
with my coals,
lick your lips with my flames,
melt you.

If I were water
I would bathe your skin,
swirl around you
floating,
carry you to the sea
with my current.

If I were earth
I would ground your roots,
nourish your leaves,
make you blossom,
be the loam
under your feet.

If I were air
I would be the cool breeze
on your face,
the wind in your hair,
the breath that
fills you with life.

ROOMS

The one where I was born
and slept in until I left home

My first one in the student squat
with the smell of dry rot

The one in a plush hotel
where we can kiss but not tell

The one in work like a cage
where we go to earn a wage

The ones I dream about
in which I am falling out

The one with the corner
when I can go no further

Those on tracks of iron
packed like passing fields of corn

The small one we hide in
to get away from the din

The one I need sometimes
to hide away my crimes

The white one we have to use
when our bodies fail us

The one where we lie in repose
until the curtains close.

READING BUKOWSKI

Under the dying light of January
he's reading Bukowski.

In the darkroom of his mind pictures
of dead lovers

haunting him,
the memory of stale cigarettes

smoking him out,
port wine staining his gut.

The devil dances at the window
the money man is at the door

and the escape is easy
down the stairwell of fantasy.

One more of those promising visions
too many hopeless ambitions.

RED FLOOR

The turned legs of the dining room table
stand four square on the red linoleum,
stretching across the room.

I remember the monthly chore
of polishing to make it shiny,
as a dancehall floor.

She, on her knees, spreading the lavender
with dextrous strokes of the polishing cloth,
waxy and cold to the touch.

I, close by, shining in rhythmic motion
using all of my elbow grease,
until I could see my face.

We polished and shone, until we could
do no more, then stood,
proud of ourselves and a job well done.

RIVERS

Rivers of blood draining my arteries
Rivers of despair pulling me down.
Rivers of tears flooding my eyes
Rivers of silence blocking my tongue
Rivers of fire burning my hand
Rivers of pain leaving me scarred
Rivers of hate poisoning my mind
Rivers of fear making me scared

Rivers of water washing my deceit
Rivers of ice slowing my decay
Rivers of stone steadying my feet
Rivers of hope paving my way
Rivers of love softening my heart
Rivers of peace helping me depart.

REMINDERS

This house is full of you.
The stacks of clothes,
useless now, to me at least,
haunt me in every room.
I smell you in the wardrobes.

After all these years, you have gone.
What am I to do with your leftovers?
Flotsam and jetsam all over the place,
hurting my eyes, reminding me of you.

I should get rid of everything
and clear you out of my life
once and for all. But I am lonely
and need you to comfort me.
Make my favourite tea.

And those shirts, idly hanging.
Perhaps, I should make a patchwork
quilt of them, for my cold bed.
To keep me warm just like you used to.

TRAINS

They arrive from every direction
like summer storms.

Sometimes they are late;
Complaints are heard.

The noise of engines pervades
like giant vacuum cleaners

and at night they are silent.
Trains like people must rest.

RETURNING

i

The completed sash windows stand
proud against the greenhouse wall,
wearing only their dull grey undercoat.
All mortise and tenon, they await
their shiny brass fittings.
Testaments to their maker's craft

ii

Sunday morning after mass
outside the friary
me in my tweed coat,
you in your Sunday suit.
Your work worn hands
weighing down on my shoulders
steadying me.
The photographer takes the shot.

iii

The day's light fades away.
You adjust and tighten the blade
of the rabbit plane with thumb
and forefinger only.
I smooth the wood, you, testing
with your palm until satisfied.
Resting your hand upon my head
 you brush the shavings from my hair.

iv

The Evening Press lies on the table
a mumble jumble of words.
Dad, I would love to read.
You sit me on your knee and
finger spelling each letter
we read the headline of the day

v

He looked up to the black sky
to the display of space
and took my hand in his.
Safe under the falling stars.
Some day, I shall leave to you,
all of this and more
and you will pass it on.

RIVER DANCE

Today the river at the back of our house
burst its banks, the water threatening
the kept grass and path.
We had moved the patio furniture.
All of us watched, enthralled by the muddy
waves lapping unfamiliar places,
splashing the garden shed, swirling around
the compost heap.
We danced and laughed fuelled
by the excitement of it all.
Soaking, we stood there
secretly hoping the water would not recede.

REGRET

When I think of what
might have been,
I feel sad

as if something lost
or stolen.

A missed opportunity,
like failing an exam
for the want of study.

Like walking through mud,
making my heavy
feet heavier.

UNFORGIVENESS

Audaciously and without a
flicker of a guilt contracting
muscle, you eye my eyes
and tell me you are sorry.

You stare me down,
death faced as if to say
so what, all of us are likely
to be found out eventually.

Guilt, like dirty windows
forbids the entry of
clear, honest light
into our sinful hearts.

What can I do now that
you have slaughtered
my defences with your
spurious apologies.

You have left me
wide open to the guilt
of my own unforgiveness.
I am defeated.

SITTING ON A RIVER BANK
watching a Ladybird climb a blade of grass

The black spotted insect
ascends, like an acrobat on a wire,
moving without waiver
until it reaches the point
where it bends the blade to the ground.

Suddenly the beautiful rounded body
is transformed into a pair of gossamer
like wings, flying the performer to
a stronger shoot, inches away.

Sitting above this ringside
of nature's circus,
I feel very small.

SOMETHING

Something is stirring around here.
You can feel it in the air, on land,
in the water. Something expected
like a long awaited birth.

The signs are there. Hearts beating
strong, smiling faces, sighs of relief.
It's as if there is a rebalancing
of the order, the untouched scales.

When it happens we shall all be
enveloped and carried like
grains of sand might be, by
a wave climbing a soft safe beach.

SOMEWHERE

Somewhere a face is falling
into a cradle of cupped hands.

A single tear is inching over
the scalded cheek of a sad face.

A voice is overcrowding
the anguished ear of a listener.

The load of the sky is pressing
down on a hunched shoulder.

Somewhere else a window has opened
to draw in generous air.

An affectionate breeze is blowing
to dry tearful eyes.

A welcome silence has calmed
a fretful mind.

A light has begun to shine.
Just enough light to see.

SONNET

Stay a while and sit with me,
maybe, we could learn something.
Stay and be my company,
perhaps, we could create a dream.
Stay with me a little longer
that we may find common ground.
Stay and our thoughts may wander
to a place where pleasures abound.

If you go, I shall be alone
and without a friend.
If you do not return
I will miss you to the end.
We are one when we are together,
Apart, we are lost forever.

SUN SALUTE

On a storm cloud morning
I sink into the floor,
stretch to the sky
and salute the sun,
ten times or more.

My cosmic greeting ended,
I slide into child's pose
and huddle underneath myself,
sheltering from the woes
of the coming day.

THE CORPSE THAT SAT IN A CHAIR
FOR FORTY TWO YEARS

She sat in her favourite armchair.
The authorities broke down the door to see who was there.
She had, apparently, just made a cup of tea,
settled herself in front of the black and white TV.

Police said there was no evidence of foul play,
the neighbours thought she had moved away.
Poor Hedviga, sitting in her thirteen square meter flat.
Nobody missed the mummified Croat.

SPACE

I open the door gently
revealing the dusty space;
the stillness of the past.

Rummaging in the half dark
I stumble over boxes of
clothes, sheets, blankets,

un-played-with toys,
a cot. The evidence of life
trapped in a loft.

I ease out of the space
careful to close the door
leaving the ghost behind.

STEPS

It's still a fresh memory for me.
That time when I photographed you
on the steps of your mother's house.
You, in your chequered dress, scuffed
shoes and your perfumed hair, wild.
You stood in front of the old door
as if on guard. Seeing that picture now
reminds me of you playing; hopping
up and down on one foot, or
taking two steps at a time
pretending to be a giant crab.
I can hear your excited screams.
I remember the garden, where
blood red Peony roses grew wildly,
throwing themselves into every fallow
space. I can still smell their fragrance.
The house, now levelled, has been replaced
by a modern building with no room
for flowers, instead, manicured specimen
plants guard the front gates.
There are no children playing there
and you are not here anymore.

SUPERSTAR

Clinging, barnacle like
your clenched fists dig deep.
Tepid water ebbing and flowing,
chlorinated blue calling us
moving as one with gentle strokes,
eying the watery reflections.

In an all of a sudden moment
you move to distance yourself.
Arms stretched, still clinging,
daring, not daring.
Slowly, your fists turn to putty,
slip sliding away, as you
find your depth.

Treading the water,
awkward, then practiced as forever
your eyes say it all.
You are the champion of the world,
aquatic superstar.
You break your hold and fall
away from me.

SURVIVOR

It was just before dawn.
I know, because the child
awoke at his usual time.
Him, guzzling milk to
quench the nights thirst.
Me, staring into the day,
the darkness rising

as out of the corner of my eye
I catch you, trespassing.
A sole survivor
of the season,
foraging, silently.
You strut, confident
of your immunity.

In a fleeting moment
you make your way through
the hedgerow to new adventures.
I wish you well,
but fear for your safety.
I feel my hold tightening
on the child.

TANGLED LINE

I am at Ferrycarraig
under the rebel hills
as the ghosts of the men of Forth
search the estuary
for evidence of invader.

With equal concentration,
I watch the rod
for proof of contact
anticipating the telling
of tales.

The smooth surface is broken
by a slithering eel,
black and shiny. It coils
my line like Asclepius' serpent
and knots itself.

For a good hour or more
I untangle line from eel,
wondering, in exasperation,
how this invader
got up the estuary.

THE GIRL WITH THE GREEN EYES

The girl with the green eyes connects
draws yours to hers, like a vortex.

You cannot escape her pull.
Her tight skin, youthful,

reflects an effervescent sheen
as she absorbs the seeing

eyes of you, stunned
at her beauty, and returned

by a sweet enticing smile.
As she passes, her wild

flowing hair brushes your face
blinding your view of the space

that she has left behind.
She floats onwards to find

and draw into her eyes
other seeing guys.

THE GROCER

The bacon-slicer on his right hand side
waits menacingly for the order.
He stands behind the counter,
white coated, ready to brown paper
the goods as required.
Bags, tins, packets and jars,
replicas of each other line
the shelves behind his head;

I have gone there many times
to find a message forgotten.
Behind the glass, at my
eye's height, rest the fresh
meats of animal and fowl
and lard, draped in muslin.
I watch, as the blade slices
wafer thin slivers of bacon.

No words pass between us
as he wraps; only a touch
of his hand as cold as meat.
He is long dead now;
Home to a bookies, the shop
still stands. On passing, I smell
the odour of freshly sliced
bacon. My hands feel cold.

UNCHANGED

Unchanged-
the black holes of the bog
scattered like traps across
the living expanse of promiscuous flora.

Unchanged –
the debris of the present
swallowed and regurgitated
as preserved history.

Unchanged –
buried deep, the memories
of secrets, of pain and prayer,
of sorrowful penitence.

Unchanged –
the purging of the past,
its transgressions, the wiping clean
of the tarnished black souls.

THE GOVERNMENT OF THE MIND

It is a Saturday in late May
and I am home, distracted, fascinated,
by the beams of light illuminating
as the sun sets its face on this house.
Elsewhere, my wife is saluting it
as my two sons build a house of clay
for the garden worms. Furnishing is required.
A flat stone gifted as a table,
a toy sheep as a pet, pebbles as steps.
The Government of the mind is ignored
in this display of rebellious imagination.

WILL ANYBODY COME WITH ME

to look for shiny shells
beside the green blue sea

to walk in the forest
under its shady canopy

to sit and ponder at
the world of natural beauty

to peel the many layers
off the face of hypocrisy

to hold the hands of those
drowning in poverty.

to bend the rules of
stagnant bureaucracy.

to uncover hidden crimes
committed in the sacristy

to lay bare the simple truth
of the houses of industry

to comfort those in the wake
of death by anomie

will anybody come with me
to set our conscience free.

THE SECOND LAW OF THERMODYNAMICS AND ME

I sit in the waiting room, queuing for the doctor,
my body telling me that I am ill.
As I hurt, I contemplate my uncertain future,
even touch on the meaning of life.
I am putting my faith in medicine
in the hope of avoiding early death.

Ah I see he is free, my saviour from death.
I make my plea- please help me doctor
I need the miracle of modern medicine.
My oh my, he retorts, you do look ill,
let me check you out, perhaps, I can save your life.
Washing his hands, he pronounces. Your future

is very much in doubt. Shocked, I reply, my future
cannot be shortened. I intend to avoid death
for many years. I have much to do in this life.
Even though you are the doctor
I have to believe that no matter how ill
I can overcome the prognosis of medicine.

He prescribed a course of medicine.
Take this he ordered, it will ease the pain in future.
Do come back to me if you still feel ill.
I peruse his bookshelf and note the volumes on death.
An everyday issue for the average doctor,
but not for me who has only one life.

I return home, to sort out my life,
clean out my pockets and dump the medicine.
I find myself wishing I had gone to another doctor,
one who would be more positive about my future.
I was fooling myself. My fate is impending death,
I just have to face the fact. I am terminally ill.

As I lumber on from day to day, feeling ill
I have come to think about my past life,
look at my dilemma and try to face up to death.
I wonder about complimentary medicine,
the final resort of anyone with an uncertain future.
I wish now I had never gone to the doctor.

No matter how good a doctor of medicine is,
he cannot protect the ill from the future.
All life tends towards death.

THERE IS NOTHING THAT CAN BE SAID
when a good life leaves its mortal bed.

No one can call back the loosened soul
after it has cut loose from its mortal hold.

No kind words can dress the sadness
of those left in the living wilderness.

No kind act can comfort the grief
or fill the gap in their disbelief.

WINTER TIME

It's late as I walk around the house
reversing time. The antique replica,

the wall plate, the heating timer
all yield as I push their hands back.

My house-mates unacquainted
with the change continue their lives.

The circulating goldfish, the perched
parrot, the sleeping dog

are not with me as I step back.
They are in my future.

As I climb the stairs I hear the parrot
whisper- careful, danger ahead.

WHERE FISH LIE

Like watery spirits they lie
deep in the black pools
suspended mid water, rising
at their whim to flirt. Teasing.

Their scaly backs flash
as they return to shelters of rock,
lying still as embalmed bodies
soaking up the silence of the dark.

WORRY
Wine undiluted dilutes worry (Ovid)

I can smell it now, a whiff of berries,
a hint of oak, soft tannins,
as I bring the tulip to my nose,

 take the first sip and fall back
to the steamy hills of Andalucía
on a summer evening.

We are watching the sunset
over Arenas, making its
escape to another place.

No time for red letter bills,
news of interest rate rises,
the uncertainty of rent.

Instead, we will hold hands,
 wander over scorched hills,
smell oranges on the wind

until we are satiated,
and insensible to any possible
worry in our broken reality.

After the Accident